AGGRESSION AND REPRESSION

In the Individual and Society

Hans E. Lauer

translated by
K. Castelliz and B. Saunders Davies

RUDOLF STEINER PRESS
LONDON

First Edition, Pharos Books, London 1981
Authorised translation by permission of the Author. Published in German with the title *Aggression und Repression im individuellen und sozialen Bereich* by Achberger Verlagsanstalt, Achberg 1975.

ISBN 0 85440 359 0

Set by PRT Offset Ltd., London N7

Made and Printed in Great Britain by
The Garden City Press Limited
Letchworth, Hertfordshire SG6 1JS

CONTENTS

Chapter One

Chapter One

DARWINISM AND SOCIOLOGY

We are living in the scientific age. Science, as it has developed from the 16th century, has led to such tremendous achievements that it has imprinted its character on the whole age. Our present culture is governed by it just as earlier times were governed by religion. Scientific methods are applied exclusively, even in humanities such as anthropology, psychology, history, sociology. These methods manifest in three different ways.

The starting point of all scientific research is observation. Its field has been continually enlarged by the invention of ever newer instruments, like the microscope and telescope which extend observation in both directions almost infinitely. The second element is experiment, which enlarges the scope of research in a different way. Under laboratory conditions experiments produce observable phenomena which normally would not occur and which are qualitatively different and can be repeated indefinitely. Thirdly all data are worked out in purely mathematically quantitative concepts. The philosopher Kant said many years ago that every science contains only as much of science as it contains of mathematics. Sociology together with the other humanities follows this pattern. Information on facts is acquired by means of interviews, opinion polls, statistics, etc. Human beings are used in experiments in many different ways. Their behaviour is observed as they work and live under various conditions. The resulting material is elaborated according to purely mathematical, quantitative terms. Anyone opening a book on sociology today might think he had picked up a book on mathematics by mistake. From the first to the last page he will encounter mathematical equations and graphs.

Indeed, these scientific methods are a distinguishing mark particularly of sociology, a science which first appeared at the height of the scientific age. It was established and given its name by the French researcher Auguste Comte in the context of his view of the course of human cultural history, which he divides into three different phases. In the first, religion was the dominating power and all natural phenomena were explained as creations or deeds of the gods. In the second, philosophy was used to reduce everything to uniform systems of concepts. In the third, the present, it is science which rules, based on sense perception and expressing the inter-relationships of phenomena in mathematical terms. Therefore sociology as the science of human society has to proceed in the same way.

On the other hand it is a fact that what distinguishes man as man and his society as human cannot be assessed by scientific methods, for it is neither perceptible to the senses nor can it be expressed in figures. Scientific methods can only measure what is physically substantial in man and society and what is held in common with other creatures. This has resulted in the belief that man is merely a *natural* being. In the 19th century the Darwinian theory of evolution denoted man, homo sapiens, as the latest and most developed species of animal. This belief is rooted as deeply in contemporary society as was religious belief in former times.

The modern faith in science has certain consequences of which only three shall be mentioned. Firstly, the purely natural beings merely exist; their behaviour is dictated by innate forces and laws but they develop no knowledge or science. By knowledge is meant man's ability to correlate ideas about natural phenomena in the form of concepts in his mind. To the extent that he can do this he understands the phenomena. If man were merely a natural being, what he calls his knowledge would be no knowledge, no certainty, but merely the outcome of his instinctive urges. Modern science actually came to the conclusion that nature, or rather what stands behind its phenomena, is beyond the limits of man's knowledge. It pays homage to agnosticism. For it, ultimate truth does not exist. According to this notion, the value of what man calls knowledge does not lie in the truth which it reveals but in its utilitarian value. Man's mental processes are the weapons he uses in the struggle for the survival of the fittest, just as animals make use of horns, teeth or claws. If this is indeed the position regarding science, then the pronouncements of science regarding man contain in themselves no real truth but are only of utilitarian value. Thus, as knowledge they cancel each other out. This puts us into the position of the classic syllogism: All Cretans are liars; therefore if a Cretan says this, he lies. His statement is self-cancelling.

Secondly, in nature there is no freedom, only inexorable laws and chance happenings. If man were merely a natural being, there would be no freedom for him either. What he calls freedom is but an uninhibited indulgence in his aggressive impulses. In fact, scientific investigation denies the existence of freedom in any form. This kind of investigation has been developed mainly in the western world, which prides itself on its 'freedom' - its highest ideal. At the entrance to New York harbour stands the famous statue of Liberty, looking with disgust towards the communist states of the East which suppress freedom. Science denies to man's intellect what to his will is his highest ideal. This brings about a split in consciousness - a sort of schizophrenia. In fact the western world today lives in this schizophrenic state. There is a contradiction between its concepts and its deeds.

This problem was the subject of considerable controversy among sociologists at the turn of the century. In science, moral and ethical judgements do not apply. We cannot call the wolf evil because he eats the lamb nor can we preach to him the ideal of a meatless diet. He has to satisfy his hunger as his constitution demands. If man were merely a natural being, social science could not apply any moral or ethical criteria to his social behaviour. It could only investigate the causes of certain behavioural patterns. This notion won the day after much wrangling. Ever since, sociology has emphasised the 'freedom' of its findings 'from (moral or ethical) values'. As far as man's social behaviour is concerned, however, this 'freedom from values' means in reality a lack of any value.

Thirdly, natural creatures are completely integrated into a whole and adapted to each other with infinite wisdom. Even beasts of prey are not a disrupting element within this whole. Were they to be eliminated, other animals would multiply inordinately. Man alone, in the course of his historical development, has emancipated himself from nature more and more and in his civilised life has created his own environment. Moreover, through modern technology he has gained an ever increasing mastery over the whole of nature, becoming finally its ruthless exploiter and destroyer. The question is: How was it possible for one single species to do this? And since through this destruction of nature man undermines his own physical existence, the further question arises: How could nature produce a creature which appears to be predestined or condemned to become its destroyer and thus annihilate itself? There is no answer to this question - and so by the application of scientific methods to the study of man, man has made of himself an insoluble enigma. He no longer knows what he really is and what his position and purpose are within the world as a whole. More than thirty years ago the well known scientist and Nobel Prize winner, Alexis Carrel, established in a book, translated into many languages, that for modern science 'Man the Unknown' still remains. Similar conclusions have since been reached by numerous other authors. It seems transparently clear that between the dominance of the purely scientific outlook (which presents man as an insoluble enigma) and the inhuman quality that modern society has assumed, there is a deep connection. As long as this outlook prevails absolutely, it will be impossible to humanise our society.

One can expose and criticise from many angles the inhumanity of present-day society, which is an outcome of this view. This is done in plenty but there is no positive alternative to offer. The most outstanding historical example is Karl Marx. He was probably the most brilliant and astute of all the critics of modern society. But his theory created the communist variety of inhumanity in place of the capitalist one.

Partly as a result of the failure of Marxism, the most perceptive minds of the last half century have been pointing out that the development of a real knowledge of man is the central task of our time. This knowledge can no longer be of a religious or philosophical nature; it must be scientific, based on appropriate experience. Therefore it is necessary to break the monopoly of natural science over the sciences in general and to found an autonomous science of man. This science would have to be based on the observation of man's inner being, just as natural sciences are based on the observation of nature.

Almost everything new that has been done in the field of human sciences in our century aims at developing such a knowledge of man. Mention is made here of only the three most important schools of thought - *Philosophical Anthropology* as developed by Max Scheler, Theodor Litt, Arnold Gehlen and others; the *Existentialism* of Martin Heidegger, Karl Jaspers and others, and *Depth Psychology* (Freud, Adler, Jung). All three have provided significant contributions.

Nevertheless it must be admitted that the only really adequate method of scientific investigation of the truly human element in man was developed and practised by Rudolf Steiner in his *Anthroposophy*. It was he who attained to the decisive knowledge in this realm. And among the fruits of his knowledge of man a new sociology developed. This has given evidence of its viability by offering the only positive alternative to our modern inhuman society - *the Threefold Social Order*. It is understandable that this idea can only be fully understood within the context of the new knowledge from which it arose. In the same way this knowledge of man depends on the understanding of the truly human element in man. If this background is not taken into consideration, the danger arises that the idea of the Threefold Social Order deteriorates or degenerates into a mere slogan, a recipe or an ideological programme.

What has so far been sketchily outlined in bare statements will be developed in the following. In order not to remain in abstract general principles, an example will be used: one phenomenon which shows the inhumanity of our present society in its most blatant form and which has currently become the central problem for sociological and socio-psychological research. This is the dual phenomenon which takes the various forms of *repression*, despotism, persecution and annihilation on the one hand, and on the other of *aggression* by individuals or groups, manifesting in violence, revolts, kidnapping, hi-jacking, bomb outrages and murders which are ever on the increase. Both parts of this phenomenon have escalated recently to such an extent that the very existence of society is threatened. Their study has lately developed into a new science, the study of conflict, to which special organisations and institutions in many countries are now devoted. The aim is to study the causes of conflicts due to repression and aggression and to find ways to peaceful solutions.

Let us consider the results of the sociological and socio-psychological research regarding these phenomena. First of all we would point out that aggression and repression did not pose any particular problems as long as the scientific Darwinistic approach to man was presented in the form developed by its founders (Darwin, Haeckel etc.) up to the beginning of this century. One reason was that society in the 19th century had not yet become as inhuman as it is today, and violent aggression had not taken on the extreme forms which it now exhibits. There were, of course, assassinations of sovereigns by anarchists, but these were isolated occurrences.

The main reason why these phenomena were as yet no problem lay in the Darwinistic theory itself. It had not only joined all creatures including man in a uniform development but had also propounded a theory of the mechanism which brought this about. How did this theory arise? In the second half of the 19th century the industrial revolution in England had led to competitive industrial enterprise. Very soon this took the form of ruthless competition between individual concerns in which the weaker went under and the stronger survived and became ever more powerful. The outcome was above all a terrible exploitation of the working classes who were forced to sell their labour on the open market at any price. On the other hand industrial mass production led to a higher standard of living for the middle classes and the profits made technical improvements possible. In short, the outcome was what one calls the progress of civilisation. In fact, the middle classes were intoxicated by it to such a degree that the idea of progress became almost a new religion. That the working classes were reduced to poverty and the weaker businesses were left behind was accepted as the price of progress. Darwin applied these ideas to nature and believed that in this way he could explain evolution and natural selection. In his major work *The Origin of Species* he mentions that he owed the suggestion to the economist Malthus. Thus 'evolution', which became the watchword of science, and 'progress of civilisation', which had become the new faith of the century, appeared to be in complete harmony.

At the beginning of our century, however, two new branches of science developed from this Darwinistic conception of man - behaviourism and depth psychology. Behaviourism did not concern itself so much with genetic connections of individual organisms as with the specific behaviour of the various species. Something specific in the behaviour of man, which had hitherto escaped notice, now thrust itself into these sciences. In most animals, the struggle for existence only occurs between species and not between individuals within the same species. The instinct of self-preservation of the species (as the behaviourist Konrad

Lorenz observes) usually sees to it that the struggle between two individuals does not end fatally. With man, however, the struggle for existence takes place between individuals. In the classical story of the fratricide of Abel by Cain it is symbolically portrayed. It would have led to the self annihilation of mankind if something else had not happened - the founding of human society. This socicty agreed upon generally accepted norms of behaviour which prohibited aggression among its members. This is not to be equated with colonies of insect species, which are collective organisms in which the single individuals instinctively perform different functions analogous to those of the different organs of the human body. Through the forming of human society, aggression between individuals is, however, only dampened down to a certain extent. The continuous succession of wars throughout human history from the days of Cain to the present time is irrefutable proof of this. The two world wars of the present century were conflicts which for the first time involved the population of all parts of the world. But this century differs particularly from its predecessors in that for the first time weapons of annihilation have been invented which have provided mankind with the technical means of collective suicide. Consequently the danger of self-annihilation has become an acute threat to future existence in spite of the social structure. In order to ward off this danger, something entirely new and decisive has to happen.

The representatives of the above-mentioned schools of thought will take exception to the denunciation of aggression as 'evil', since aggression is an inborn, natural instinct in man as in other creatures and cannot be cut out with the surgeon's knife. All one can do is build dykes to channel the aggression so that it does not overflow like a mountain torrent in flood, devastating fields and meadows. Or, to use another metaphor, one can construct safety valves through which the steam of aggression can escape without causing an explosion which would destroy the mechanism of society. What, then, is to be done in practice?

Let us first review what social psychology and behaviourism have to say about the forms of aggression and repression which have appeared in the course of human history. These fall into three categories.

The first and oldest can be classed as sublimation. It is recognised by the fact that the aggressive urge, though provoked, is immediately diverted into paths where its expression is raised from the material world to the spiritual and becomes refined and sublimated. In this way it is transformed into the capacity to create cultured civilisations. One need only call to mind how the high culture of Greek antiquity was achieved by applying the principle of *agon*, of contest, in all spheres of life. The most famous example is the Olympic Games, in which in olden times the contests were not only gymnastic but also poetic and musical. The highest flowering of Attic tragedy and comedy we owe to the contests of dramatic poets. In a similar way the knightly tournaments of the Christian Middle Ages gave aggression scope to express itself, but these were so ordered by rules that the virtues of knighthood could develop. There is also the well-known legend of the song contests in the Wartburg. Finally, in these past ages, those who directed their aggression not against their fellow men but against the evil and baseness within themselves were canonised and revered as examples for others to emulate. This can be compared in the present age with the awarding of honours in academic competitions. In place of the saints of the Middle Ages we have Nobel Prize winners.

A second form of aggression, which can be classed as perversion, developed later, especially in political societies. It arose through the fact that not only codes of behaviour but also convictions developed and were prescribed. It followed that non-conformists, people with different views, or, above all, critics, were branded as enemies of society; they were persecuted, punished and exterminated by fire and sword. In these acts, aggression could assume the most inhuman forms and even earn thanks, recognition and respect, since it was performed in the service or at the command of society. Thus aggression became perverted by society into repression of the individual. This does not contribute in the least to the advancement of civilisation but - when it is ripe so to speak - leads usually to revolutions, that is to mighty upheavals of the political order leading to civil wars. The most infamous example of this repression was the persecution of heretics by the medieval church, which saw itself as God's kingdom on earth. Hundreds of thousands were sacrificed at the stake. This ended with the religious revolution of the Reformation and finally led to the atrocious religious wars of the 16th and

17th centuries. Further examples of this phenomenon may be seen in what preceded and followed the political revolutions of 1789 in France and 1917 in Russia.

Finally a third form of aggression, which can be classed as frustration, developed in modern western industrial society. The principle of this society is to give rein to the free play of aggression in the individual, but by its own nature this has led to society repressing the individual. Competition forces the individual to be aggressive if he does not want to go under. Since the build-up of economic enterprises has reached the point where the majority of those involved are in subordinate positions, the individual is under such pressure from above that the degree of aggression forced on him from outside usually far surpasses his normal aggressive urge. He cannot give vent to it in the manner and degree corresponding to his nature. Thus he is frustrated. As a result of this frustration illnesses of mind and body develop (nervous disorders, coronary diseases, depressions); or, as with many young people, the urge to escape from society leads to vagrancy, drugs and suicide.

So what can be done in face of this state of affairs?

The social psychologist Alexander Mitscherlich observed that the frustration of the individual caused by society is harmful to both. Since life in modern society is more and more determined by technology, its repressive domination of the individual takes on the character of compulsion by technological systems and their manipulations. In the age of cybernetics and automation, industrial society is developing a life of its own which is no real life but the mechanical running of a machinery which takes less and less account of human needs and living conditions. Moreover, it destroys its own natural environment and heads for self-annihilation. To escape this fate, aggression by the individual towards society must be released and animated, albeit not in a destructive but in a constructive way, by allowing for objective information and free criticism, for complaints and protests against inhuman behaviour and destruction of the environment, and for popular movements for reforms etc. In this way society can be saved from the rigidity of technological industrial compulsions and can retain its flexibility and capacity for transformation and so be spared total collapse.

Konrad Lorenz sees the demands of the future in a somewhat different way. According to him the frustrated, obstructed aggression of the individual should be relieved by more leisure for sports and games of all kinds extending to artistic activities on the stage and concert platform; for only thus can health of mind and body be re-established so that man can withstand the menace of industrial society. Only in this way can aggression be sublimated, enabling a new culture to develop.

However both Mitscherlich and Lorenz admit that it cannot be guaranteed that either way the collapse of our society and its final self-destruction can be avoided. All that can be hoped for is that these recommendations might lead to a relatively optimal result.

The characteristic of the whole of sociological and

socio-psychological research is that it does not deny that modern western industrial society is based on a fundamental aggressive urge, for it considers this urge to be a natural instinct in man. It seeks to contain it within limits or to mitigate the results by compensatory activities which balance it. Since it does not seek to counter aggression with an opposing force, the question remains whether the form which aggression takes, enhanced and strengthened by the technology governing our society, will after all be stronger than the recommended remedies, and win the day. This is what is so unsatisfactory in the results of this kind of research and why in recent times another line of thought has arisen which will be considered in the next chapter.

Chapter Two

Chapter Two

PSYCHOLOGY AND SOCIOLOGY

Another line of thought of sociological study has more recently appeared in opposition to psychoanalysis and behaviourism. In a sense, this runs parallel with the trend of science today, as exemplified for instance by Walter Heitler in physics, by Adolf Portmann and Ludwig von Bertalanffy in biology, by Arthur Jores in medicine and Arthur Koestler in philosophy. In sociology it is represented by Richard Behrendt, Josef Rattner and others. In a recent collection of essays entitled *Making of Human Aggression: A Psychological Approach* edited by Herbert Selg, a group of young sociologists decisively contradict the line of thought described in the previous chapter. The tendency of all these efforts is to reveal, more clearly than has the attitude of natural science, the special place which man occupies in the whole of creation. To this extent these sociological studies have contributed to the realisation of the central task of our century - the elaboration of an adequate comprehension of the whole nature of man.

In the field of sociology this tendency is noticeable as an underlying idea in the works of several authors who maintain that aggression is not an inborn instinct in man but has only been acquired in the course of historical development and can therefore in the progress of time be overcome. In other words: if aggression exists between individuals, this is not a primary characteristic that distinguishes man from animal but merely a secondary one. Seen from another point of view, man's life changes continually in the course of history while purely natural creatures have no history and live in endless repetitions.

This poses the question of how, in the course of history, aggression arose. Josef Rattner in one of his latest works *Aggression und menschliche Natur (Aggression and Human Nature)* pointed out that this had been answered long ago by the psychologist Alfred Adler. His many years of preoccupation with the phenomenon of aggression led to the formulation of his theory of depth psychology. He considered that aggression arose from the central characteristic of man - his capacity to be culturally creative and live in the flow of history. But how is this in turn to be explained? Adler maintains that it is obvious from a mere glance at the difference between the life of an individual animal and that of an individual human being. The animal is born a relatively completed creature endowed by nature with instincts and all the capacities necessary for life. These begin to function shortly after birth, and the animal's maturity, which coincides with puberty, is achieved relatively early. From this point on it begins to age, though for some time imperceptibly. Nothing new develops. By contrast, man is born altogether unfinished. All his specifically human capacities, such as upright posture, speech, thought, memory, self-awareness, are only present as potentialities and have to be developed and come to fruition through the effort of learning over a long period of time. Only as a grown-up person does he complete this to a certain extent - but however old he becomes, he is able, if he makes the effort, to acquire ever new capacities. No one can claim to have developed all of man's potentialities. Man is simply an unfinished being. Since he has to develop his capacities in an individual way, he is able to use them in different ways and to varying degrees and create thereby ever something new and different. Thus he becomes culturally creative, whereas all the individual animals of a particular species respond to their instincts in the same way.

The fundamental 'unfinishedness' of man, in contrast to the finished animal, can, of course, also be regarded as the imperfection of man in contrast to the perfection of the animals. Adler maintains that primitive man saw himself as an imperfect being compared with nature and the perfection of all its creatures. This aroused in him a deep-seated feeling of inferiority in comparison with the rest of nature. To overcome this he felt the urge to develop his potential capacities. But how to set about it? He noticed that the creatures of nature maintained - and probably attained - their abilities through the struggle for existence, that is the search for food, defence against enemies, and the killing of prey. So he set about imitating them by fighting his human competitors, rivals, enemies, in order to weaken them, conquer them, subjugate them and make them serve him. In consequence he became aggressive and at the same time he developed his varied and latent abilities to create culture.

Three forms of aggressiveness may be distinguished. First there is the aggressiveness of an individual against his fellow men. From this proceeds monarchism in its various forms, chiefdom, tyranny, monarchy, all of which existed in olden times. In the maintenance of their power, the leaders developed certain abilities which made them appear as demi-gods or heroes and a cult grew up around them.

Secondly, Adler sees the aggressiveness of tribal or social groups against one another. This led to class distinction and class rulership which existed the world over in ancient times. The few (oligarchs) who attained such dominance over the many thus developed certain higher faculties and felt themselves to be better and nobler (aristocrats, noblemen) than the mass of their subjects.

Thirdly there is the aggressiveness of whole nations against other nations. This led to foreign rulership, to imperialism, that is the founding of empires as in the old Oriental civilisations. Gradually the ruling nations gained the idea that they were called to the task of world rulership. All nationalism as well as militarism are seen as the outcome of such accretion of power. What arose in these various phenomena through aggressiveness gradually became tradition, habit and, finally, a sacrosanct and immutable social order.

Today we have reached a point where, through science, technology and international commerce, mankind as a whole has been welded into one common civilisation in spite of being split into political and military power blocks. The earth has shrunk, so to speak, into a single city - a megalopolis - and all its inhabitants have become neighbours. Under these circumstances every local conflict threatens to spread to global proportions. If we wish to survive, we are forced to observe a universal truce which cannot be subdivided. Into the bargain our century has presented us with weapons of destruction which make it possible for mankind to annihilate itself. As a result of adherence to the traditional aggression between the different groups of humanity, these weapons have been stock-piled to an extent which would allow us to exterminate ourselves many times over. They are being multiplied continually at a cost of about 200,000 million dollars per year. In view of the increasing threat to our very existence these armaments can only be seen as sheer lunacy. For Rattner one of the main tasks of the future is to make the voice of reason heard, which would oblige us to establish world peace. The other task he sees as the development of a feeling for human community and an awareness of each individual's responsibility. He concludes his above-mentioned book as follows: 'Therefore forms of education, of cultural and political control must be devised which will erect impassable barriers for power-thirsty and megalomaniac politicians, who in pursuit of their crazy machinations threaten to plunge the whole world into destruction. Most people never think of going to war. At the outbreak of war they usually have to be compelled to take up arms and kill or be killed. The only hope for mankind is that the voice of reason and the feeling for community will make itself felt more and more. To the extent which awareness of the need for solidarity grows among people, social sense arises and gains influence.

If we are to continue to live in an undivided world, it will have to be a world of peace.'

These trains of thought, and the solutions they offer, seem very plausible, just as are those referred to in the first chapter. But in both cases they are merely half truths, and leave one dissatisfied. First, there remains the question as to what form the 'new systems of education and cultural life' should take. The last chapter of Rattner's book only goes so far as to mention that in contrast to the traditional authoritarian order of government, militarism and chauvinism, they should be of an anti-authoritarian character. But it may well be doubted whether the voice of reason in the realm of politics and sociology would be listened to and would carry more weight in the future than it has in the past. From this past, however, there rings in our ears the familiar postulate of the Swedish statesman Axel Oxenstjerna: 'With how *little* reasonableness is the world governed!' And if ultimately education towards community feeling should be insisted upon, there is the danger that, if it is not undertaken voluntarily, it will be forcibly imposed, resulting in repression of the individual as practised in communist countries. The opposition between the two above-mentioned tendencies of sociology and social psychology, and the solutions offered regarding the phenomena of aggression and repression, correspond in a certain way with the contrast between western and eastern forms of social order.

What, however, is the deepest reason for the inadequacy of these proposed remedies. It is that both lines of thought, though in varying degree, are unable to escape from the scientific Darwinistic image of man. In Freud and Lorenz this is abundantly clear. How else but by seeing man as merely another species of animal could Freud have made a dogma of the theory that the libido, the sexual urge leading to the reproduction of the species, was the driving force of the human soul? He called this urge the 'Life Force' because it is aimed at the reproduction of life. In his later years Freud added as a second driving force the death, or destructive, urge which can be identified with aggression. Human life appeared to him as the expression and - at the same time - the battlefield of the eternal, irreconcilable and unresolved conflict between these two urges. 'This conflict is the fundamental content of life and the development of civilisation can be described in short as the struggle for life of the human species.' Thus was man reduced to a mere living organism, for every organism contains in some form or other the conflicting forces of birth and death.

Alfred Adler and his followers do indeed emphasise the difference between man and animal. But on the basis of what they call specifically human characteristics they too cannot explain the aggressive urge. For an explanation they are obliged to fall back on the aggressiveness natural to the animal world. And so Darwinism creeps in, as it were, by the back door. The struggle for existence, supposedly observed by primitive man in the animal world, was in reality only projected into it by Darwin. For primitive man, on the contrary, nature in all her manifestations was ensouled and indwelt by lower and higher divinities. Nature was divine.

In the following chapters the scientific view of man as presented by orthodox sociology will be contrasted with the science of man founded by Rudolf Steiner, with reference, however, only to those fundamental findings which have a bearing on our special subject. First, though, let us regard for a moment the third school of depth psychology, the complex psychology developed by C. G. Jung, which to a certain extent can build a bridge to Steiner's school of thought because, of all modern theories, it comes nearest to it. (See *C.G. Jung und Rudolf Steiner* by Gerhard Wehr). It has furthermore developed concepts in psychology from which a real solution to the problems of aggression and repression could be found. Jung himself did not formulate such a solution because on the one hand he was not concerned with social problems to the same extent as Freud and Adler, and on the other hand he was unable to fill these concepts with an entirely satisfactory tangible content.

What all three schools of depth psychology have in common, justifying their collective name, is their concern with the unconscious depths of the human mind, or more precisely, research into the relation between this and the phenomena lying more on the surface of consciousness. The point of emphasis, however, lies in a different place in each of the three schools. For Freud's psychoanalysis this is the *unconscious*. The reason is that it places man nearest to the animal and therefore considers him as one of a species. This is expressed, as we have said, by the fact that psychoanalysis in its initial stage saw the sexual urge, which serves the reproduction of the species, as the fundamental urge of human soul life. This urge has a special relation to the unconscious. The sexual act is often called 'sleeping together', and in earlier times was probably consummated in sleep. For Freud the unconscious constituted the principal realm of soul life. Consciousness centred in the 'ego' is only a peripheral phenomenon. Thus he calls the core of man's psyche not an 'I' but an 'it'.

In Adler's individual psychology the point of emphasis lies, on the contrary, in the realm of *consciousness*. He sees the unfinished in man, his capacity to learn and therefore to transform and develop himself. In every process of learning, man proceeds from a position of not-knowing, i.e. unawareness, to one of knowing, i.e. awareness, and since the process of learning is individual, this awareness takes on the character of awareness of self, which includes all that is connected with its development, such as egoism, aggressiveness and also pathological abnormalities. Hence the term individual psychology.

In Jung's school the emphasis is placed equally on the *unconscious* and the *conscious*. The significance of its investigation owes its character to what is derived from both sources of soul life. This school had the advantage of being able to work from the foundations laid by Freud and Adler. As with Adler, the conscious is centred in the ego, and this ego-consciousness implies a separating of oneself from the surrounding world and one's fellow men. On the other hand, the unconscious, as in psychoanalysis, has a collective character, though in a different sense. While for Freud the collective character is based on the bodily nature and the perpetuation of the species which overflows in the sexual urge, for Jung it is rooted in the soul itself. He develops the idea of a collective soul which embraces the unconscious part of every man's soul life. One could therefore maintain that man, because he directs his consciousness towards his ego-centre, develops 'anti-social instincts' which, if multiplied to excess, lead to aggressiveness towards his fellow men. On the other hand, through belonging to a collective human soul in his unconscious, he develops 'social instincts' which, if they increase to excess, lead to the repression of individuals. One could point out that a free society through the study of the sciences would encourage the awakening, i.e. the 'becoming conscious' of the individual, while on the contrary a dictatorial repressive society would endeavour to maintain him in a quasi sleeping condition. The contradiction is perpetuated in the way information is handled in the two systems. If man were able to weld together the two sides of his soul life, he could bring aggression and repression into balance so that the conflicting instincts are neutralised.

And herein lies the other side of the significance of Jung's school of thought. Here, too, the human soul appears as something in the process of development and transformation. In this development three stages are distinguished. At first the soul is an undifferentiated unity. In the second stage it branches into a day-side and a night-side, the realm of consciousness and the unconscious. In the final stage, when its development has reached its goal, it once more becomes a whole, thus achieving the 'self' (which Jung differentiates distinctly from the 'ego' or centre of consciousness). It is true that Jung's concept of the self lacks a tangible content. He was of the opinion that, in the unification of the conscious with the unconscious, the consciousness of the soul sinks back to an intermediate dream-like state of half consciousness. This is why he maintains that the self could be developed by a special attention to and schooling of the dream life. It is also why the possibilities, inherent in his psychological concepts, of mastering aggression and repression could not be developed into fruitful ideas.

Chapter Three

Chapter Three

THE SCIENCE OF MAN

In characterising as briefly as possible the science of man developed and applied by Rudolf Steiner, and called by him Anthroposophy, a distinction has to be made, as in every science, between *subject,* i.e. he who practises it, and *object,* i.e. what it is about.

In natural science the subject is man, the object nature. The object is *outside of man.* The object must be given to the subject for the latter to experience it and so produce science. This happens in natural science through observation by means of the senses. Historically the victorious progress of natural science thus began from the moment that sensory observation became the determining factor in research. The results of scientific research are arrived at through man pondering on the content of his sensory observations.

In the science of man the subject is man, and the object - is also man. Both are the same. The subject matter is man himself - self-knowledge. Here too the object must be given to the subject to experience it. Since they are both identical, i.e. man pondering over his experience, the point of departure of this experience cannot be external and sensory; it must be the inner, *mental self-observation of thinking man.* This is actually the only door through which to approach the study of a true science of man. It is as it were the 'eye of the needle' through which everyone must pass who would enter. And here again the results of research are arrived at by pondering over observations.

However, self-observation is, as Steiner pointed out, not immediately possible for modern man. There are two reasons. Firstly, man in this scientific age has become so thoroughly and one-sidedly accustomed to the observation of the outer world through his senses that the capacity of inner self-observation is almost completely stunted. This has reached its extreme in our century through the effects of the mass media which flood man ceaselessly, day after day, from morning till night, with visual and aural sense impressions. Secondly, in the process of thinking, man is, in the truest sense of the word, active. He is, however, not immediately in a position to perform an act and at the same time observe this act from the outside. This only becomes possible if he raises the intensity of his thinking activity far above its usual level. Such an intensification of thinking can be achieved by a method of schooling which Steiner once called, by way of comparison, mental gymnastics. As muscles can be strengthened by certain regular exercises over a period of time, so can the intensity of thinking be significantly heightened by certain regular repetitive exercises of thought over a period of time. These consist of thoughts or acts of thinking which, at one time or another, open the door to a sudden knowledge, a revelation of a truth. It is not enough to recall the particular truth every time; the train of thought which led to the experience of understanding has to be recreated again and again. One can take a thought of one's own choice or ask the advice of someone who is experienced in such matters. In this way the power of thinking is strengthened to such an extent that one starts to perceive it inwardly as an activity actually while doing it. What does this teach us?

From many possible examples one experience may be selected which, though appearing trivial at first, is of tremendous significance. This is the fact that when thinking we all move in the same sphere. To give the simplest example: 2 x 3 = 6 or 3 x 4 = 12 are true statements for every one of us. It might be argued that this only holds good for the realm of numbers, and that in many another field the thoughts of different people are decidedly contradictory. This is indeed so. But why should it be different in different fields? The reason is that with regard to the relationships of numbers people's feelings are in no way engaged, while in most other spheres their sympathies and antipathies, their wishes and desires influence and determine their thoughts without their being aware of it. To the extent to which people can exclude these influences from their thinking, forming their concepts calmly and impartially instead, they are able to come to agreement even over the most difficult problems. At the same time we also come to another realisation - namely that in the world of thought the same conditions prevail in *one* particular respect as in the sense-perceptible world. We can only observe an object from one side at a time, from the front, from behind, from right and from left, gaining each time a different view which has to be combined with the others in order to discover the total truth about it. In the same way every concept we form of a thing gives in reality only one aspect of it and must be complemented by other often contrary concepts in order for the whole truth to be grasped. These different concepts do not actually contradict each other but illuminate the thing or matter in question from different sides. They invite us to discover from which viewpoint they were seen. Their real significance is revealed in their relation to these viewpoints.

The capacity to grasp the truth about a thing in this way is inherent to a greater or lesser degree in everyone. Through this capacity we gain what we call 'knowledge'. By this is meant that through it we make present in our conscious mind, in the form of concepts, the relationship between phenomena according to their own inherent laws. This faculty is a specific characteristic of all human beings. But the faculty itself, and what it enables a person to achieve, is not inherent automatically, nor does it fall to everyone in the same way, as do the instinctive faculties of animals, but must be acquired by each person through individual effort. Each achievement or discovery in the field of knowledge is first made by *one* man with whose name it remains linked. We speak of the Pythagorean theorem, Aristotelian logic, of Kepler's planetary laws, Mendel's laws of heredity, and so on. Yet these discoveries do not *remain* personal properties. On the contrary, once they are made public anyone is able to follow these thoughts, and so the discoveries become the property of mankind. Metaphorically speaking, the individuals concerned are the instruments which serve mankind in the acquisition of a particular portion of knowledge. This is why the 'copyright' for every creation in the sphere of the mind becomes the common property of mankind very soon after the death of its originator.

This is one aspect from which the *fundamental difference* between man and animal can be seen. The difference lies in the relationship between *species* and *individual*. The individual animal is interchangeable with every other member of its species. In all its characteristics and capacities it is determined by its species. It has no freedom. It is not the individual specimen, but the species to which it belongs, which is interesting. Is it a sparrow, a tit, a finch, a swallow? In man, however, what is contained within the species has spread out and entered into the single individual, who unfolds it in an individual way which occurs but once and is never repeated. The way he does this is left to *him*. In this sense he has the potentiality of free determination. This demonstrates the *freedom* of man not only as fact, but it reveals the true nature of the idea of freedom. It is based on man's possibility to determine in which way he will release that in him which is universally human. At the same time it can be seen that this occupies a *middle position* between two opposing poles. One of them is *necessity*, which exists when the single creature - as with the animal - is entirely determined by the characteristics of the species. The other is the *arbitrary caprice* of one who fulfils his potential at the expense of his universally human qualities.

This can be illustrated by comparison with the musical composition of a 'Theme with Variations'. In the species of the animal kingdom there are *themes* pure and simple which are repeated by the individual animals without variation. In contrast, individual human beings are always *variations* on a theme. Each one is different from any other, yet the same theme underlies them all. If the underlying theme cannot be detected in one of the variations, the composer can be said to have acted arbitrarily instead of composing in inner freedom.

Through all this the mystery of the human individuality is revealed. A man is not only an individual - he is at the same time an individual realisation of what is universally human. This mystery is penetrated ever more deeply as progress is made on the path of knowledge of the science of man.

It has been mentioned that the human being to-day is in general only fully conscious as regards his *sense impressions*. This consciousness refers to an 'ego centre', i.e. he is aware that the sense impressions are his own. However, what he calls his 'ego' is only a dark spot within his consciousness. It has no content of perception. One might object by saying that its content is the sum of memories that it can call up from within. But these memories reflect no reality, only impressions received from the outer world.

Thinking as an activity lies, as has been said, beyond the threshold of consciousness, in the unconscious, though it borders immediately on this threshold. The inner perception of thinking means raising it to an inwardly widening consciousness (which can be achieved by strengthening it through meditation as described).

Feeling belongs to a still lower level of the unconscious. Only when very strongly aroused will its waves rise to the surface of consciousness. But normally it remains in the unconscious. A second important step in pursuit of the science of man is the schooling of the whole realm of feeling through meditative exercises which are repeated in such a way that certain distinct feelings are aroused in the soul intentionally. Active work in one of the fields of art can be of great help to this. The actor who plays a certain part, the musician who performs a composition, has to find his way into the appropriate mood. By such schooling the life of feeling can also be lifted up into the light of a widened consciousness.

A third and last step on the path described here is a particular schooling of the *will*. The will constitutes the deepest and darkest layer of the unconscious and is so bound up with desires that it cannot be clearly distinguished from them. It can, however, be parted from them if a schooling is undertaken in which certain acts of will are regularly repeated which are not called for by any outer circumstances but are the result of a free decision. In this way the will can be strengthened and released from the realm of desires to such an extent that eventually it will be revealed to conscious inner perception. Then the consciousness will have been so widened that it encompasses the whole soul nature, and the experience of 'ego' will have gained a hitherto unperceived content. What is this content?

Supposing a person on a journey meets 'by chance' someone who subsequently has a decisive influence on his life, be it as friend or foe. If, through the schooling described, he has been able to raise his will from unconsciousness into consciousness, he will become aware that this encounter was no accident but was, though unconsciously at first, sought by him in obedience to a decision made by his ego before birth. This awareness is possible because, together with the lower levels of soul life, memory also is lifted up (through the schooling described) into consciousness that goes back before birth and reaches ever further into the past. Eventually his memory shows him a situation in which he was together with the other in a former incarnation on earth. This former shared experience led to the prenatal decision to meet again with this person in this life, in order to experience the result of their former relationship.

In short, the central discovery or experience on the anthroposophical path of knowledge is, in the end, that of *reincarnation*. It implies that every individual is involved in the whole historical development of mankind, since he or she incarnates in every epoch under ever changing conditions. Everyone goes through this development in an individual way, assimilating the achievements of humanity in the course of its historical development, each in his specific way. Every person is not only a member of the people, profession, race and century in which he is embodied during a particular incarnation but is moreover a member of all the peoples, professions, races and centuries in which he incarnates in the course of his development. This knowledge gives the fullest deepest significance to the fact that an individual is not only an isolated personality of one single life but is a realisation of the universally human.

To this basic knowledge of the nature of the human individuality we have to add that of the nature of *mankind.* Every species of animal has its own special environment from which its form and its whole mood of life can be understood. A bird does not make sense without the air in which it flies. Nor a fish without the water in which it swims. There are animals of the desert, of the forest, of the high mountains and of the lowlands in the various zones of the earth. What is man's particular environment? He is the only living being who has spread over the whole earth, who dwells in all places - all continents, mountains and plains, forests and deserts. He has conquered the sea in ships and the air in aeroplanes. One could say that *the whole earth with all its zones, continents and elements is his native environment.* Recently he has even walked on the moon, since which time this, too, belongs to his environment; for were man only an earth being, he would neither have felt the urge nor developed the capacity to reach the moon. But did the moon only become part of man's environment at the time of the first landing? It would have been impossible to land on the moon if exact details of its distance, composition and orbit had not first been known. So it must have been part of man's environment even earlier. What about the whole planetary system? The knowledge of its underlying laws, its organisation and movements, which we owe initially to Kepler, would never have been discovered by man if they had not been part of his environment. The same holds good for the fixed stars in view of the discoveries of modern astronomy and astrophysics. *So actually the whole universe must be seen as man's environment out of which he is fashioned.* Thus in olden times he was called the microcosm, the 'world in miniature'. Aristotle maintained that because the human mind in principle embraced everything in the world, it was indeed 'everything'. And modern philosophical anthropology has discovered man's limitless 'openness to the world' (Max Scheler) as his specific distinguishing mark. In this sense mankind's universality is to be seen as its basic characteristic.

Some might object that this conception implies a regression into ideas of antiquity and even older times, long since outgrown. The geocentric cosmos of the Greeks was based on the position attributed to man as the centre of the universe. Sun, moon and stars circled around the earth, man's dwelling place. Sigmund Freud once spoke of three deep injuries inflicted by modern times on man's awareness of his human worth. The first occurred when Copernicus placed the sun in the centre of the planetary system and relegated the earth to the periphery as just another planet. Thus man was robbed of his central position in the universe and degraded to merely an inhabitant of this planet. One can understand the total rejection of the new theory by the guardians of the traditional image. This injury was aggravated by modern astronomy when it revealed that the central position of the sun and even our whole planetary system, in which Copernicus still believed, is an error and recognised that our central orb is only one among thousands of other suns within a limitless universe of stars and galaxies. With this the earth with all its inhabitants finally shrank to a mere 'speck of dust, within the vast immeasurable all.

The second injury to man's former awareness of his humanity - according to Freud - was inflicted by the Darwinian Theory of Evolution. This destroyed the religious belief that man was created by the hand of God and revealed instead his animal origin, his descent from ape-like creatures.

The third injury man received - said Freud - was inflicted by his own theory of psychoanalysis, which showed that it is not man's 'ego' who is master in the house of his soul but the world of desires of the unconscious 'id'.

Of all these 'discoveries' it can be said: If the situation were really as they suggest, then they could never have become 'knowledge'. Here too the comparison with the Cretan holds good: when he says that all Cretans lie, the truth of this statement invalidates it. At best they can be allowed as half truths in the sense discussed earlier of being a one-sided aspect of reality. The other aspect is found in equally solid facts.

Firstly, through the modern astronomy inaugurated by Copernicus, man has more than ever before shown himself to be not only an earthly but also a cosmic, universal being by transferring the viewpoint from which he observes the universe to extra-terrestrial realms; first to the sun and later to the fixed stars and the galaxies. Secondly, following the Darwinian theory of man's derivation from the animal, Nietzsche first saw the possibilities for man in future to ascend the ladder of evolution, becoming 'super-man'. Modern biology aims to achieve this by means of genetic engineering. Thirdly, at the same time that Freudian psychoanalysis established the rulership of the unconscious over the 'ego' in the house of the soul, Steiner's Anthroposophy inaugurated a method for schooling the powers of the soul by means of which the conscious ego is able to exert its rulership over the realm of the soul's unconscious.

Thus we see as the two main characteristics of humanity on the one hand man's potential *individuality*, and on the other his potential *universality*. So it is not surprising that the recognition of these facts opens up quite a different view of the phenomena of aggression and repression from those sketched in the previous chapters. In the following we shall endeavour to outline what the consequence of this new outlook could mean for the ordering of social life.

Chapter Four

Chapter Four

THE DIALECTICS OF HISTORY

In the first two chapters, the implied criticism of the scientific, Darwinistic picture of man does not mean that the theory of evolution as such is denied; rather the interpretation given to it by Darwinism with its exclusively natural scientific mode of thought is challenged. The consequence of the mechanistic character of this interpretation was to make man appear as a mere accidental product of the evolution of nature. Anthroposophy, too, sees man as a result of cosmic evolution. Since the whole universe is man's environment, his form and organisation are expressions of the combined influences of all the formative forces of the universe. How this view is arrived at can be found described in Steiner's work in many ways and need not be repeated here. Instead we will give a brief summary of the development of man - since he emerged as man - as seen in the light of Anthroposophy.

This development falls into three main epochs, of which the major part of the final one belongs to the future, though its distinctive characteristics are already clearly foreshadowed in the present. The triad of epochs comes about because of the two main characteristics of man, universality and individuality, are not developed simultaneously and constantly. The first epoch is characterised by *universality* and the second one by *individuality;* the third is destined to bring about a *synthesis* of the two. The evolution of man takes its course in the three steps of a dialectical development in the manner outlined by Hegel. The universality of man constitutes the thesis, the individuality the antithesis, while the third epoch will have to realise the synthesis. From another point of view these epochs represent the development of body, soul and spirit, whereby these three concepts receive a specific content from the three principles mentioned.

The salient feature of the first of these epochs was the principle of universality, particularly in the development of the bodily nature. This epoch embraced many thousands of years of prehistory and came to an end round about the fourth millenium B.C. With the invention of writing, chronology and the calendar, mankind then stepped into the historical phase of his development. Even in astrological and alchemistic literature of the late Middle Ages there are descriptions of the human body, originating from older times, in which it is seen in twelve parts corresponding to the twelve constellations of the zodiac: the brow - Aries; the organs of speech - Taurus; the arms - Gemini; the chest - Cancer; and so on down to the feet - Pisces. The twelvefold zodiac, through which the sun and planets pursue their courses, appeared in the old days to comprise the totality of all the creative forces of the cosmos which produced their microcosmic image in the human body. And as, according to the then current ideas, the sphere of the fixed stars constituted the outermost sheath of the world which enclosed the seven planetary spheres, so the human form enclosed the inner organs which correspond to the seven planetary spheres - brain to the Moon, lungs to Mercury, heart to the Sun, gall-bladder to Mars, and so on.

This conception is to be found in a different form in the creation myths which have come down to us from early cultures whose spiritual vision was directed mainly back into the past ages of prehistory, for instance in Genesis, the first Book of Moses. In this book of the Bible, the first main epoch is pictured as the paradisial existence of man. It was in existence in a world which in itself was an all-encompassing whole: divine-natural, heavenly-earthly, spiritual-corporeal. In it stood man in such a way that he, together with all other beings, was intimately linked in all-embracing archetypal unity - with Divinity who spoke to him, with the animals which surrounded him, with the trees which grew in the Garden of Eden. Even he himself was an undivided whole containing both sexes. For Adam and Eve are, in the biblical sense, not to be seen as single individuals but as symbolic images, pictures of as yet undifferentiated humanity which, owing to the blood-relationship of its members, felt itself as one body, though membered in two sexes. Only thus can it be understood that the original sin perpetrated by mankind's archetypal parents could have consequences for all their descendents. The sin of Adam and Eve was the sin of all mankind. Only in times when the language of myth was no longer understood could the idea arise that the Fall was the purely personal affair of Adam and Eve with no consequences for their descendents. From this followed the controversy between Pelagius, who held this idea, and St. Augustine, who maintained that the

Fall was plainly the cause of the corruption of mankind.

The mythical stories should not be interpreted as successive events in time relating to definite years and days. Rather they portray allegorically the inner quality of events without indicating a quantitative passage of time. The Fall and consequent expulsion from Paradise are in reality pictures of the transition from the first to the second main epoch of human development which extended over many millennia. The process of individualisation, which set in with this transition, is characterised in Genesis in two ways. Man developed his own will which enabled him to disobey God's command. He was cast out of Paradise, that is he lost his original bond both with God and with nature. The curse with which God expelled him: 'Cursed is the ground for thy sake ..... in the sweat of they face shalt thou eat bread', means that nature will no longer nourish him like a babe at her breast, but that he himself has to earn his livelihood through laborious toil. And differentiation takes place not only in relation to man's cosmic environment but also within his own human realm. The slaying of Cain, which belongs to this sequence of events, shows the human race differentiating into contending individualities. In the books of Moses only one passage points to the fact that the Fall entailed by the original sin does not end till the dawn of history with the story of the Tower of Babel and the confounding of language. Again it is man's presumption in rebelling against God which drives him to build a tower reaching up to heaven, and this time he is driven out of the paradise of the one primal language into the desolation of the multitude of tongues.

We must, however, not imagine that in the passage to the second main epoch of development mankind lost the quality of universality. Rather, it appeared in a new form. The connection with the divinity which, in its previous form, had been broken, was re-established in a new way through the founding of religion. By means of prayer, sacrifice and ritual it was continually maintained. Likewise the connection with nature was re-established in a new way through agriculture and animal husbandry, which enabled man to produce with her help what he needed for his bodily existence. Also the relationship between individuals took on a new form through the emergence of an organised society. This did not arise from practical considerations to prevent self-annihilation, but was, rather, a new form of what had existed before. Over a long period of historical development, the new achievements continued to be permeated by the principle of universality. The spiritual life was dominated by religion, material existence was governed by agriculture, and in their social relationships individuals still felt themselves entirely as members of communities. Only gradually did the principle of individuality increase to a strength which brought about a balance of power between individual and society. Even in ancient Greece, in approximately the middle of known history, though the names are known of many individual personalities, such as statesmen, generals, poets, artists, who through their deeds or creations have achieved lasting fame, yet the importance of the community stood above that of the individual, as is evident from the practice of ostracism in the city states. Persons who had won high esteem through services rendered to their city were banished for five or ten years in order that their influence over their fellow citizens should not become too great, though they had committed no offence and did not suffer any loss of respect.

Only when the Roman state was expanding to become the Roman Empire was a *complete balance achieved between the individual and society*. (Jaspers calls this period the 'axis' of history because in a sense the whole of history turns upon it). On the one hand the Romans, the most gifted political and military people of their time, gave the state (which represents universality) the most perfect form. On the other hand constitutional law was balanced by the civil law which established the civil rights between man and man, thus creating for the first time a private sphere within the framework of the law in which the individual was free to live his own life. The most important of these laws were those concerning private property. They enabled the owner to do what he liked with his possessions without considering anyone else, even controlling it posthumously by the provisions in his will and testament. This new conception of property contributed considerably to the Roman citizen's feeling that he was a free, independent, self-determining personality.

So in Rome, for the first time, human relationships were divided into public and private spheres. This principle of duality is characteristic of the Romans. For instance every official post was occupied by two officials. A symbol of this principle can be seen in the cult of the god Janus. The first successor of Romulus, the founder of the city of Rome, Numa Pompilius - the initiate among the seven kings of Rome - changed the year of ten months into one of twelve months and dedicated the first of these to Janus. In this two-faced god the Romans saw a symbol of what they felt was characteristic of the human being; one face looks at us as a civic community, the other as an individual. The first embodies the principle of community or universality in which people are united through peace and love; the latter, the principle of individuality or isolation which leads to conflict and war. Christian historians later saw this duality even in the name of the city. Read in one direction it spelled 'Roma' which in accordance with its Greek origin signifies martial strength, and read in reverse the word 'Amor' pointed towards unification in civic communities united by love. Indeed, it was political unity of the ecumenical church of the Roman Empire, as it was then, that made possible the spread of Christianity.

Proceeding with history beyond the fall of the Roman Empire one comes to the Christian Europe of the Middle Ages. The Germanic tribes which, during the migration of the peoples, flooded central, southern and western Europe and settled there, had for a long time remained in a sort of childhood state. They only fully entered into their historical development with the migrations, and repeated in one millenium in their own fashion what the oriental peoples had been through in a different way over a period of two thousand years. Thus during this time conditions developed which were analogous to those that had existed in the old Oriental civilisations. Once again the spiritual life was represented by religion, now in the form of the Christian Church, while material life was governed by agriculture. Only in the second half of the Middle Ages, with the flourishing of the townships, did crafts and trades acquire importance equal to that of agriculture. Within the purely human sphere, governed by Teutonic law, public and private life were not yet separate. The form of government arose both from the theocratic situation and (as feudalism) from the agrarian economic structure. Finally the supremacy of the principle of universality came to expression once again in the dominant position of the Holy Roman Empire whose ruler considered himself Emperor of the World and thus successor of the Roman Caesars.

With the dawn of the modern age the new European peoples had reached a stage of development comparable to that achieved by Graeco-Roman antiquity. As the old Oriental cultures were recapitulated during the Middle Ages, so from the 15th to the end of the 18th century was classical Antiquity, and this found its expression in the various movements of the Renaissance which followed each other in Italy, France and Germany. Part of this Renaissance consisted in the reintroduction of Roman civil law. From this originated the first purely secular states in the new Europe. Of course the circumstances were not the same as in Roman times. Historically the mission of the Germanic peoples and their successors was to bring to fruition the principle of *individuality* in its purest and therefore most one-sided form. The predisposition to this has shown itself since the beginning of the modern age with elemental force. The state of equilibrium between individuality and universality achieved by Rome became a state of *imbalance* again but in the opposite direction to that of pre-Roman times. The emphasis now lay in the element of individuality. This has been expressed ever since in the drive towards freedom, i.e. the free self-determination of both individuals and peoples, which has become the ruling principle of life.

In the sphere of spiritual life this was made manifest on the one hand in the Reformation. In the new ecclesiastical organisations arising from it, the intolerance of the church of the Middle Ages was replaced by religious liberty and freedom of conscience. On the other hand the same impulse gave birth to modern natural science which, in contrast to medieval philosophy - the 'handmaid of theology' - was not accountable to any authority, but only to the sense of truth and conscience of the individual scientist.

In the field of political life the new spirit of the times also manifested itself in two ways. Firstly, the new purely secular states embodied the principle of universality no longer in the truly human sense as in Graeco-Roman antiquity, but in a national sense only. They became states each of which represented the general interests of a particular nation. Since the new peoples which developed to maturity during the course of the Middle Ages were, above all, language communities, the states which they formed each made its own into its official language. Thus cultural life (science, literature, poetry), which depends to a large extent on the medium of language, was led away from its former ecclesiastical sphere more and more into the region of secular administration. The right to self-determination became an over-riding political ideal of modern times, and absolute sovereignty the jealously guarded requisite of every nation. With this the principle of individualism intruded into the sphere of common life, i.e. that of the principle of universality. This is a kind of repetition in the political sphere of what happened in the cultural sphere as a result of the Babylonian confusion of tongues. Symbolic of it was the decline of the Holy Roman Empire which occurred parallel to the rise of the nation-states.

To counterbalance the overweening individualism and egotism of the nation-states, Hugo Grotius in the 17th century postulated an 'international law' as a comprehensive universal element of justice. But in spite of the later founding of the Court of Justice in The Hague this never became binding. Finally, in the present century following the First World War, the League of Nations was set up as the first universal political organisation for the purpose of settling inter-state conflicts by peaceful arbitration. After its early demise, the United Nations Organisation was founded with the same aims following the Second World War. It still exists, but from the beginning was condemned to complete impotence, which has lent impetus to endeavours aimed at setting up a world state or world government. This remains wishful thinking and has no chance of being realised so long as the principle of individualism holds sway unchallenged.

The second form in which, since the beginning of the present age, individualism has shown itself in the political sphere, was, in contrast to ancient Rome, the new political science which was introduced in England by Thomas Hobbes in the 17th century. According to this, before the states came into being there was a 'pre-state' epoch in human development which had the character of a war of all against all. To put an end to this, the single individuals united together by means of a social contract in which they recognised their mutual rights under the protective umbrella of a state. It follows that the state is a creation of man, an instrument made to serve *his* interests. At first this new idea was a mere theory, though a theory which could even justify the absolutism of the monarchies of its day. However, it held the seed of a parliamentary government which emerged at the end of that century after the Cromwellian revolution, and later spread throughout the world.

Chapter Five

Chapter Five

THE PRESENT SOCIAL CRISIS

The transition from the 18th to the 19th century marks the transition from the recapitulation of Graeco-Roman antiquity, that had been taking place during the previous three centuries, to modern times. At that point the principle of individuality reached its zenith as regards both the shaping of social life and the relationship of man to the universe.

In the political sphere one of the factors in this development was the growth of the parliamentary system or, as it was called, 'free democracy' which, as mentioned earlier, took place in England in the 17th and 18th centuries. It is the form of government by which the varying or opposing legal claims and commercial interests of individual citizens make themselves felt in parliament, which is the legislative representation of the people. This takes effect through the struggle for power between political parties, and through their periodic alternation as government and opposition. Starting from England in the 19th century, this system commenced its triumphal progress through the world.

Another factor in this development was the declaration of human rights as formulated at the birth of the United States of America. These human rights included all the different freedoms that individuals in equal measure may claim as the natural rights with which they are endowed at birth. They are therefore rights which - according to Hobbes - existed prior to the political state, and which the state, through its legislation, merely has the duty to express as legal rights. Freedom and equality were both postulated as rights, to be put into practice in free democracy. These declarations of rights were formulated anew during the French Revolution, and the French Republic which was proclaimed after the fall of the monarchy was built on the principle of equal rights for all citizens.

The most important change at this time, however, was in the realm of economic life and was due to the industrial revolution which, significantly, occurred in England in the last third of the 18th century. It was nothing less than the principle of individuality flooding into economic life, for through the ensuing industrialisation competitive private enterprise appeared. In this the impulse of freedom was given its most powerful and far-reaching character. Together with the mass production arising out of industrialisation, it gave such an impetus to economic life that in the course of the 19th century the economic sphere became the most important and dominant aspect of society. Since that time we have lived in an industrial society, and when the western world speaks of freedom or free society, it means, on the whole, free commercial enterprise.

However, it must be said that freedom also started to suffer its most fateful deterioration within the commercial sphere. In the third chapter it was pointed out that the freedom which is an integral part of man has its roots in the human realm, in the specific relationship between the individual and the species. It can only be understood when seen in this relationship, and can only be achieved to the extent that this relationship is realised. If the pattern of life is determined by only *one* of these poles, freedom deteriorates. When the individual is the sole arbiter, despotic egotistic lust for power is the result; when the opposite is the case, freedom is extinguished in compulsory subjugation.

The extremely one-sided development undergone by the principle of individuality in modern western society has perverted freedom into arbitrary egotistic striving for possessions and power, i.e. the urge to aggression. Thus it can be said, in agreement with individual psychology, that this urge has arisen in the course of history; not however, as an imitation of animal aggression, but out of the nature of man himself, as a result of the extreme, one-sided emphasis of that one of the two principles inherent in him which belongs to the second main epoch of his development. Free commercial competition thus soon took the form of ruthless rivalry, and so, at first in the economic field, began the war of all against all which Hobbes thought had been brought to an end by the founding of national states. Or rather, to be precise, this war now for the first time turned from hypothesis into historical reality. Adam Smith characterised, and thereby more or less sanctified, the egotistic pursuit of profit as the legitimate motive for all commercial undertakings. An 'invisible hand', he believed, directed individual enterprise inspired by egotistic profit motives towards the attainment of the greatest common good. For when every individual looked after his own interest in the best possible way, then the interests of the many were also best served. In reality, by being conducted in this way economic enterprise was estranged from its true purpose, which is the serving of actual consumer needs. Production became an end in itself, no longer supplying the needs of the consumer but having as its sole purpose profit for the producer. The constant striving towards expansion in order to make profits became its fundamental tendency. This tendency led, in the 19th century, to a new wave of colonialism, for new colonies provided ever new sources of raw materials for industry and new markets for growing production. Britain's colonial kingdom grew during this time into a commercial empire. France, Belgium, Holland and Germany expanded into colonial nations.

The alienation of industry from its real purpose not only resulted in a constant expansion of production, but also led to a new class structure in society with a new ruling class. The representatives of industry - the owners of the means of production, the 'capitalists' - became the ruling class. The place of former divine or priestly kings was taken by steel, automobile, bank and oil kings. The mere consumers, the professional and academic classes, the government officials, and - the largest group of all - the industrial workers, sank to the level of governed subjects. True, the industrial workers were involved in production, but they were not reckoned as producers since they did not own the means of production. They merely sold their labour to the entrepreneur on the labour market for an agreed period according to the principle of supply and demand. Since, in the 19th century, supply generally exceeded demand (craftwork was less and less able to compete with industry), the price of labour, i.e. wages, could be forced down to a minimum subsistence level. Thus a new form of slavery arose - wage slavery - which brought in its train the utter destitution of the industrial worker.

Conditions were intensified in the extreme by the fact that the industrialism which started in England as free commercial enterprise spread, at the beginning of the 19th century, all over Europe. Amongst Europeans, the French are the people in whom the spirit of Rome still works on most strongly. Thus France was the first country to take on Roman law. Seen through the eyes of Roman law, free enterprise, having discarded the state control prevalent in the time of absolutism and the mercantile system, must needs appear to belong to the private sphere. Therefore the need arose to regulate this sphere, too, through appropriate laws, as was indeed achieved during the consulate of Napoleon in the *Code Civil,* the first modern code of civil law, which subsequently found its way far beyond the borders of France. It implied, fundamentally, acceptance of Roman civil law with the old Roman concept of private ownership as its central norm. This was applied to something which did not exist at the time of ancient Rome - industrial means of production, i.e. capital in the modern sense. Thus industrial or capitalistic industry became private enterprise, which meant that the owners of the means of industrial production could lawfully do what they liked with these, for their own material advantage, without regard to the consequences for the common good. Besides this, modern society (as in ancient Rome) was divided into two distinct spheres, private and public, which had, however, acquired a new meaning. The private sphere, to all intents and purposes, became identified with industry, and the public sphere with the state which, as the modern state, has also assumed responsibility for cultural matters (education, research, etc.).

Now industry in this position was not only at variance with the true purpose of production - the satisfying of existing consumer needs - but also with the very nature of industrialism itself. From the social point of view what distinguishes it from agricultural and craft production is the principle of the division, that is the specialisation, of work. This happened not only within industrial organisations but between one enterprise and another, between one industry and another, even between countries, so that what up to then had been national economies became fused into international world-wide commerce. The result was, on the one hand, that industrial production became a matter for communities of varying sizes, and on the other that the consumer, individual or collective, was no longer able to satisfy his needs with the produce of his own labour but depended to an ever greater extent, and eventually completely, on outside supplies from world production on the international market. This situation runs counter to the fact that the means of production, according to the Roman concept of private ownership, are private property over which the owner can exercise an arbitrary right for his own interest and profit, and to the fact that the proceeds of the common production flow into the pocket of the owners while the worker is only paid according to supply and demand on the labour market. Apart from the fact that in this way society becomes split into a class of owners and a class of workers, an all-powerful monied class and a class of exploited have-nots, the consumer is in principle at a disadvantage in relation to the producer.

The outcome of all this was that from the middle of the 19th century the socialist movement started to arise out of the economically and legally disadvantaged industrial proletariat. This movement has as one of its aims the replacement of the egotistical profit motive by the social ideal of mutual support and as another the overcoming of the existing class structure and the creating of a classless society. The Marxist theory gradually attained the leading position within this movement. It aimed to reach its goal by making the means of production common property through state ownership and by substituting state planning for free enterprise.

In the Russian Revolution of 1917, Lenin brought into effect a socialistic ordering of society in accordance with this recipe. It soon revealed itself as a complete failure. Marx considered the dictatorship of the proletariat as indispensable during the transition to the new order, but in Russia this dictatorship was assumed by the Communist Party as representative of the proletariat. The state of affairs persists to this day and so, instead of a classless society, a new class rulership has been erected. Those wielding power are a small minority of the Party and their subjects are the vast majority of the rest of the population. In place of the multiplicity of private capitalists in the West, there is the state, i.e. the Communist Party, as the sole universal capitalist which, besides owning the means of production, also has total political power through controlling legislation, government, the armed forces and the police. The alienation of production from its true task of satisfying consumer needs did not come to an end but only assumed a different form. While profits in the West, apart from what is spent on living in comfort, are invested in expanding production, they serve in the Eastern bloc the consolidation of power of the rulers over the ruled, as well as the extension of the world-political power of the communist state. Thus, since the founding of the Soviet Union, the primarily economic imperialism of the West has been countered by a political, ideological imperialism in the East. For a quarter of a century these two have been engaged in a cold war which has led to an armaments race the like of which the world has never seen.

The Soviet failure to solve the social question left the majority of western workers deeply disillusioned. They merely put up with private capitalism as the lesser evil. A number of circumstances have certainly made this easier, however. For one thing, the social legislation of previous decades had already ameliorated the lot of workers as regards their rights and their economic position. Furthermore economic life was given a tremendous boost by the enormous amount of reconstruction needed after the Second World War and the necessity to make up lost ground. There was full employment which, on the whole, has continued to this day. Millions of foreign workers were engaged to satisfy the labour requirements of the western industrial nations. As a result of all this, the workers in western industry have acquired a power almost equal to that of the employer. Industry and the whole of western society is now in the phase of what is known as monopoly capitalism. What is the significance of this?

It is the culminating intensification of the one-sidedly developed, that is egotistic, principle of individuality in the relationship of man to man and man to the universe. Industrial production has expanded and burst all bounds. At the same time industrial and with it social power has become concentrated within an ever smaller ruling circle. A few gigantic concerns and financial institutions control world economics. In place of the former contrast between capital and labour in the western world, we have today the contrast between the wealthy industrial nations which live in luxury and the developing countries of the Third World where poverty and hunger prevail. As during the course of the last hundred years the exploitation of the workers in Europe led to socialistic revolutions in various forms, so the exploitation and destitution of the Third World, which marks the society of our century, is leading towards a world-wide revolt of the former colonial coloured peoples against the ruling white race.

Hand in hand with the enormous increase in production goes an ever accelerating advance in technology, especially nuclear energy for both industrial and military uses, the computer's invasion into all fields of human activity, the development of space travel and the explosion of the information industry through the mass media. The advancing mechanisation of our whole life leads to ever new constraints. These turn the 'free' enterprise of the West more and more into a technically planned economy and increase the pressure on all those engaged in it. Thus the dominating position of economics within society aggravates the repression of the individual by the system. Furthermore technology is increasingly replacing man by machines and forcing him into conditions which destroy him body and soul. The consequences are physical and mental illnesses, the many forms of escape from society, or opposition and aggression against its institutions and representatives.

While in the late Middle Ages the emphasis within economic life was on the craftsman, and during the epoch of mercantilism on trade, it has now shifted to industrial production. As industrial production has become ever more determined by technology, man has been losing the connection with nature which he had during the period of agricultural and handcraft production. He has made himself lord over nature, even exerting his egotistic will against it, thus becoming its exploiter, poisoner, polluter and destroyer. So he has now reached the point of destroying the very basis of his physical existence.

Within the western world the state has become the servant of economics and the instrument of industrial growth. In addition it embodies national egotism and world-political aspirations to power. Global society, represented by the United Nations, is condemned to impotence vis-a-vis the conflicts of the national states and those of the super-powers.

Cultural life - thanks to the freedom it gained in the religious sphere through the Reformation and in the realm of knowledge through the founding of modern science - has abandoned the world of the divine, with which it had been united by religion, and increasingly turned to material nature. Knowledge has become increasingly identified with science. The resultant conflict between faith and knowledge which flared up in recent centuries has been settled now by the victory of knowledge. The relation to the divine was completely severed and atheism began its reign. In the materialistic world conception which science has fostered, the material world is the only reality. As a consequence man's consciousness has undergone a change. From being a child of God in olden times, he became the most highly developed animal, i.e. a mere creature of nature. Since in nature there is no freedom but only necessity and chance, this implies that he sees himself as an accidental product of evolution and, in principle, negates the existence of his freedom. What he used to call 'freedom' is now revealed as merely the uninhibited expression of aggression which he has in common with other species of the animal kingdom, even though it appears in a different form. Does not the modern economy, indeed the whole of society, offer irrefutable proof of the truth of this? Clearly this aggressive instinct was let loose in the most unrestrained way in economic life - for this was concerned with tangible possessions and solid profits. In the scientific, cultural and creative realms this was generally less so. Aggression did not pay in these realms as it did in economic life. For those engaged in these professions, the so-called freedom recently achieved therefore gradually lost its value. Finally, during the 19th century they relinquished it 'voluntarily' and subordinated their work increasingly to government administration. Thus education and research became more and more subject to political ends imposed by the administration. When in the 20th century the state itself succumbed and became the servant of economics, they fell completely under government control. Scientific research today is largely concerned with the technical development of armaments and with the growth of industrial production. Education is there to prepare the manpower and specialists needed by industry, making the greatest possible use of available talents and ensuring that even at the pre-school stage there are equal opportunities to climb the income ladder. Thus freedom in the cultural life of the so-called 'free' western world today means little more than it does in the communist east.

In this way, through one-sided development of the principle of individuality pushed to its extreme, modern man has completely emancipated and isolated himself from the natural, material world as well as from the divine, spiritual world. He feels himself cast into a cosmic vacuum - into nothingness. At the same time, partly through aggression and repression against each other, and partly through the practice of destroying the material basis of existence, men are threatened with self-annihilation. Man's development has thus reached the critical point at which it will be decided whether he is to flounder or whether he will reach his goal.

In this situation, what proposals has social science to offer? On the one hand, as suggested in the first chapter, it recommends mitigating and moderating the repressive authority of those in power by releasing the frustrated aggressiveness of the individual and directing it towards the criticism and reform of industrial society; in other words dividing the aggressiveness of modern society into opposing forms of expression which mutually keep each other in check.

On the other hand, as suggested in the second chapter, there is the call to set against the madness threatening our society - through unchecked aggressiveness of man against man and against nature - the voice of reason which demands indivisible peace and a feeling for community and shared responsibility.

Neither of these suggestions will suffice to turn the tide, for, as pointed out in the introduction to the first chapter, modern science, which as exclusively natural science governs our present-day cultural life, has made of man an unanswerable enigma with regard to his inner nature, his origin and the meaning of his existence. As long as this remains it will not be possible to give to society a structure really worthy of humanity. The only effective remedy for the present crisis can be a methodically sound science of man which can provide genuine answers to the questions about his real being and the meaning of existence. This leads us back to the description in the third chapter of a science of man which has actually been established in our century. In the following chapters it remains to be shown how this can help to overcome the social crisis, in that it points to the ordering of society necessary for survival and further development.

Chapter Six

Chapter Six

INDIVIDUAL AND SOCIETY
A DYNAMIC SYNTHESIS

One of the primary fundamental truths arrived at by the science of man developed by Rudolf Steiner as a method of research is the discovery that in the kingdom of man it is inherent in the individual to realise in a uniquely individual way what is universally human. This is the mystery of the human individuality, and the profundity of this mystery is revealed through an understanding of the law of reincarnation, which states that every individual in the course of his incarnations not only takes part in the evolution of mankind but also assimilates the results in his own unique and unparalleled fashion. As stated earlier, this evolution takes place in three main phases. In the first there is in the bodily aspect a factor of universal unity in the mode of life of mankind owing to the dominating influence of blood-relationship. In the second, man as a soul being develops himself into a self-determined but at the same time isolated individual. In the third, ultimately through the knowledge of reincarnation, he finds in the depths of his own self the universally human element as the spiritual core of his being. Thus the synthesis between individuality and universality is attained - man's essential achievement and at the same time the final perfection of his being. So full self-knowledge and the realisation of one's full potential are inseparably connected. And the full realisation of freedom is synonymous with both, for it is nothing other than the manner in which a person determines, in his own individual way, the realisation of the universally human within himself. This means that the ability to attain freedom is recognised as a fact and its true nature defined.

To bring about this three-in-one consisting of the true knowledge of man, of a realisation of genuine freedom and of the synthesis of the principles of individuality and universality must be (at first predominantly in the cultural realm) recognised and tackled as the central task today and in the future. Without knowledge of what man is and how he fulfills his nature no humanising of society is possible. As in past centuries the methods and results of science gradually became common property, so in the coming centuries the path of knowledge and the achievements of the science of man must, in their fundamentals, become common property. This means not that natural science should be replaced by the science of man, but that this should be included as a necessary complement. It does, however, mean that the accepted monopoly of the scientific approach in natural science must be broken and the overstepping of its legitimate boundaries be checked. This task of the cultural realm is an inescapable necessity even in the light of its own development, as evinced by the succession of the contrasting cultural forces of religion and science. The new science of man (as will be shown) will provide also a synthesis between these two.

How can this task of the cultural realm be fulfilled in the coming centuries? Here we come to the second element of the above-mentioned trinity - freedom. Man's propensity to freedom is not only a fact recognised by the science of man under discussion; by working at this science man actually attains freedom. The schooling for spiritual self-awakening, which is the method of this science, can only be accomplished by free decision, and to maintain it requires a daily renewal of this decision. As one becomes aware of the universally human in one's own self one is transformed as of necessity into a representative of the universally human, and this is identical with the achievement of freedom.

It is therefore obvious that the future task of the cultural realm can only be realised to the extent that it is set free in its entirety, i.e. that it becomes autonomous as a separate sphere of society. Only thus can it be released from its slavery to the state and to economic considerations, and redirected towards its true objective. So long as it is under state control this is not possible, for the powers which today dominate the state are interested not in a knowledge of man and realisation of what is truly human, but only in political power and economic profit motives. For this reason, they have no use for autonomy in education or research. It is feared, too, that chaos and fragmentation would result, for everyone engaged in this sphere would surely ride his own hobby-horse, which would lead to irreconcilable conflict between the various ideas and directions. This fear is understandable in a world which, as has been shown in the previous chapters, no longer knows any freedom but only the aggressive instinct. It can only be overcome when the cultural life, especially education in its widest sense, is oriented according to a true knowledge of man. Only this would make it possible to transform aggression into the exercise of freedom and allow the aims of education to arise from the nature of man and the needs of his development. Obviously there is an interdependence between the spreading of this science of man and the freeing and final autonomy of the cultural life. Just as the science of man needs a free cultural life in order to reach its objective so a free cultural life needs the science of man upon which to establish itself in a suitable form.

The humanising of society can only begin when the members of the rising generations are brought up through their education to be true human beings. The interdependence mentioned is demonstrated convincingly by the world-wide educational movement of the Rudolf Steiner (Waldorf) schools based on the insights of Anthroposophy. These schools, which are free from administration by the state, are a vigorous source for what could become an autonomous educational system. They work not in a confusion of pedagogical theories and practices but with a basic curriculum varied according to local needs and circumstances. This curriculum is not laid down by an official body. It describes what is needed for different ages and subjects according to insights into the human being and the requirements for his development gained from the science of man elaborated by Rudolf Steiner. Thus the rising generation can unfold its full potential. The curriculum helps the teacher to map out his path according to his capacities and yet remain free in his teaching. It is the only educational movement which, in its fifty years of continuous existence, has achieved a transformation in education which has borne fruit both pedagogically and socially. This was only possible because it is based on Anthroposophy, the science of man.

The second step on the path towards a human society involves the other side of the achievement of freedom, which entails the acquisition of a true knowledge of man. It is indeed an act of freedom to endeavour to redeem this freedom from its present-day perversion into egotism and aggression. If genuine freedom consists in the realisation of what is universally human by the individual in his own individual way, the resulting bearing and attitude is not ego-less but 'ego-strong', is not selfish but selfless, for it draws its aims and orientation from all that is universally human. True freedom is therefore not anti-social but social; it furthers human relationships. In his early philosophical work *The Philosophy of Freedom*, with which he laid the foundation for Anthroposophy, Rudolf Steiner wrote: 'To *live* in love towards our actions, and to *let live* in the understanding of the other person's will, is the fundamental maxim of *free men* . . . Were the ability to get on with one another not a basic part of human nature, no external laws would be able to implant it in us. It is only because human individuals *are* one in spirit that they can live out their lives side by side . . . The free man does not demand agreement from his fellow man, but expects to find it because it is inherent in human nature ...' This quality of truly free deeds will develop all the more as an understanding of the laws of reincarnation grows, arising from the inner schooling described. The destiny of every individual in the course of his incarnations is inextricably linked with the destiny of the whole of mankind and depends on how *this* is decided. *The individual can only achieve his appointed goal if the whole of mankind also achieves its goal.* Knowledge of this cannot but make him rise above all selfish desire for possessions and lust for power, giving him a feeling of responsibility through his actions for the destiny of all mankind. This sense of responsibility will then govern his attitude and behaviour.

In the terminology of Jung's psychology: The transformation which thus takes place means that the individual ego of normal consciousness melts into the collective unconscious in the process of 'reunification'. Jung describes this as the true process of individualisation through which man while developing his 'self' completes the realisation of his being. The collective unconscious is nothing other than the immortal individuality which passes through the succession of incarnations and represents the universally human in the individual. Jung's path from the 'ego' to the 'self' is therefore the path towards awareness of the true reincarnating ego. Thus each single person in his own way becomes a 'representative of mankind'.

This points to the source from which alone a true social renewal of the present anti-social economic life can flow. Communism has shown that nationalisation is definitely not the answer. Today, as social-political literature confirms, even the western world has come round to the view that a socially and environmentally favourable form of economy will only be possible to the extent that *new values* are found, new moral impulses are born and the whole of life is given a new meaning by a 'new philosophy'. But mere appeals to reason, or moral preaching, will not suffice. Ways to knowledge through inner activity must be opened to man so that he may acquire deeper insights which of themselves are transformed in his soul into moral strength and social attitudes. By way of a comparison, Rudolf Steiner used to say that a stove cannot be persuaded to heat the room by being told that that is its moral duty. Just as the stove must first be filled with wood and coal and then lit, so a human being must first be given knowledge if he is to act in a moral and social way.

If such a step could be achieved, industry would not have to be nationalised in order to lose its unsocial character. It could remain independent, 'free', and yet become socially satisfactory. In fact if this is to come about it will have to be protected from state interference (currency manipulations, market control). What does it mean to 'socialise' industry and commerce? It means to restore it to its proper function, namely the satisfying of real consumer needs by production and distribution of the requisite goods and services. To begin with, to mention only the essentials, it will be necessary to form associations not only of people engaged in production and distribution, but also of *consumers* according to their different needs - food, clothing, housing, transport, energy, etc. These consumer associations would have to be in constant contact with those of the producers and distributors in order to negotiate the quantity, quality and price of goods and services necessary for the maintenance of a material existence worthy of the human being. Instead of a 'free' market economy or a bureaucratic state-controlled economy, a 'third way' is open - an economy so organised that its three main functions of production, distribution and consumption work in constant co-operation. In addition it will be necessary not to nationalise the means of production but to find a metamorphosis of ownership in keeping with the true purpose of industry. Since production will become the concern of integrated communities which in turn are engaged in providing for the needs of the whole of mankind, the ownership of property will have to be transformed into stewardship, with corresponding obligations towards all those engaged in industry and commerce, guaranteeing that each enterprise serves the common interest in the best possible way.

Industrialism as 'free' enterprise was originally fully justified. Division of labour meant that the managers and the workers co-operated. The manager required freedom for organisation, initiative, planning, personnel management, etc., as does everybody who works in the professional and creative sphere. Originally he had this freedom by means of owning the means of production, for the owner and the manager were one and the same person. But because there was no adequate concept of freedom, and because the Roman concept of the private ownership of an enterprise was employed, the entrepreneur came to consider himself more as owner than manager. So freedom deteriorated into egotism and authoritarianism. In place of service to the consumer, control over the subordinates and interest in profits developed. If the ownership of the means of production were to be transformed and developed into legally constituted stewardship, then the freedom needed by the manager could remain and be put to the service and welfare of society.

If the creative and cultural sphere can become free, and industrial life be made social, then society takes on a human face, for the life of society will then have the same structure as will the single individual in the third phase of human development. This structure has been described as the synthesis of the principles of individuality and universality. In the individual this equals the fulfillment of his real humanity. It reveals itself in the balance between freedom and social impulse. This balance swings rhythmically between absorption into the inner self and devotion to the society of one's fellow men. These are interdependent, each requires the other. Both solitude and sociability are part of the life of the individual when it is truly human.

The life of society is shaped in a similar way. In it the synthesis of individuality and universality (which make it human) is expressed in the alternation between differentiation into individuals who work in the creative, cultural sphere, and integration into social, co-operating groups in the economic realm. These again are interdependent, the one requiring the other. Cultural life developing in true freedom will not lead to egotism and authoritarianism of the individual but to a moral and social urge to be active in brotherly collaboration in the economic field. This in turn will not result in repression and exploitation of the individual, but will provide a standard of living which will allow him to take part in cultural life in full freedom according to his interests.

What is new in this development is the discovery and unfolding of 'universally human' aspects in the individual and of individually human aspects in society. It could also be said that a new 'Romanism', transformed and raised to a higher level, is needed for the future.

As mentioned earlier, in ancient Rome history had reached the point where the principles of individuality and universality had gained a state of equilibrium. This was expressed in the way the whole of life was governed by the legal sphere which was divided into the two aspects of private and public rights. These two, as representatives of the individual and the universal, stood rigidly and statically side by side. Within this framework man as individual and society as the state confronted each other. The clear-cut separation ensured that the tendencies of aggression and repression were kept in check.

When Roman law was reintroduced in recent times the former duality was transformed into that of private capital or privately owned industry on the one hand and the nation-state on the other, which absorbed and administered the cultural life. As in the course of western development the state, and the cultural life it dominated, degenerated into the servant of the economic sphere, which became the ruler of society, the aggression on which the economy (as private enterprise) is based turned into repression against the individual. The result is the crisis threatening the life of modern society.

What the future needs is the synthesis of the principles of individuality and universality in a state of dynamic functional balance, and this synthesis is needed equally within the individual and within society. In both cases, however, its synthesis is realised in three different ways: in one way in the cultural sphere, in another way in the sphere of the state and the rights it safeguards, and in a third way in the economic sphere. To make this possible the administration of society has to be divided into these three spheres. The following diagram illustrates this.

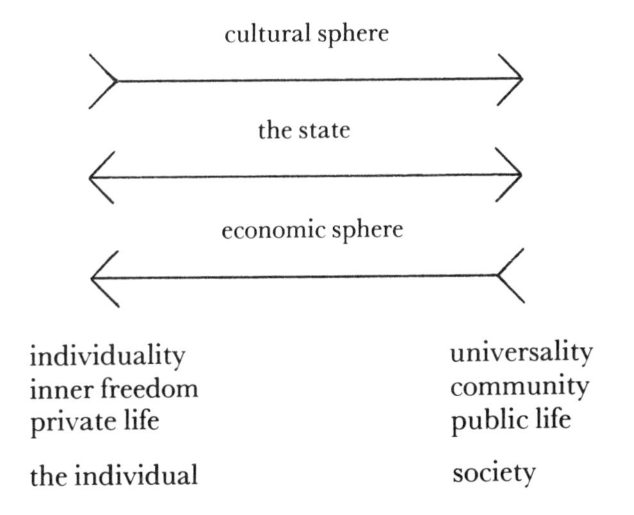

The cultural sphere has its roots in the private realm. The individual must be free to choose his cultural interests according to his abilities and aims in life. This must be his private affair. The fruits of culture, however, are of public concern. The institutions and creations of education, science, the arts, religion and information will no longer be the privileges of the elite classes, but should benefit everyone.

Conversely, the industrial economic sphere has its roots in the public realm. As production has become the concern of larger and larger groups, it must be so organised that it satisfies the consumer needs of all mankind. It is no longer the private affair of the producers. The fruit of industry, however, its consumption, is the private affair of the individual and must be left to his free choice according to his personal needs.

Finally, the state represents equally and simultaneously the interests of the individual as well as of the community. It has to formulate the rights of the individual in the cultural, legal and economic realms (freedom of conscience, the right to education, the right to vote, the right to satisfy basic needs, etc.), as well as its own rights and spheres of competence.

All this goes to show that the division into private and public realms corresponding to the individual and the state must be relinquished, because both these realms are present in all three spheres of society. Schools which are not state schools are then not private either; they are public if they are open to everyone. And that commercial enterprises are by nature public has been recognised even in western capitalist society by the fact that railways and other transport, post and telecommunications, the production of gas and electricity, have been nationalised, i.e. placed under public administration. In principle the same applies to the food and clothing industries, etc., as became clear during wartime shortages when the state took over the control of distribution.

The division of society into the three spheres is not an anatomical division, it is a functional arrangement of society in which the three interpenetrate, though each is active according to its particular principle.

Finally it is evident that within the threefold society the state occupies a fundamentally different position from the one it holds in the present society. It is no longer the representative of the principles of universality but rather in a special sense the mediator between interests of the individual and society in general. In this way it becomes the sphere of rights and laws. In the final chapter this will be taken a step further.

Chapter Seven

Chapter Seven

THE SOCIETY OF THE FUTURE

The previous chapter offered a description of how, through the new knowledge of man, a new and truly human social order arises. This was characterised as a metamorphosis, in a certain way, of something which had existed in the Roman Empire. It was shown that in the new order the state acquires a new position and significance within society as a whole.

In ancient Rome an equilibrium had been achieved between the principles of individuality and universality. It came to expression in the fact that in place of religion (theocracy) and agriculture the realm of legal rights was the dominant element in society. This realm fell into two spheres - private and public (state) life. The first embodied individualism, the second - universalism. When in more recent times Roman law was re-established, it created the duality of the national state and private enterprise, which is the distinctive mark of modern society; because the state (public sphere) was conceived of as only national and the private sphere was identified with commercial activity. In the present century this duality has been split into the opposing social systems of the West and the East which for the last quarter of a century have been engaged in a cold war against each other.

In the West the state has become the servant of capitalistic private enterprise which, as free competition, is founded on unrestricted aggression. Here the emphasis is on the private sphere. The private wealth of the representatives of industry stands in contrast to the impecuniosity of the state especially when it comes to financing cultural life. Even public transport is more and more being pushed to the wall by private means of transport.

In the East the former national state became the instrument of power of a socialistic ideology, which took the place of the former national culture. This new state took over the administration of the economic sphere. Through nationalisation the private sphere was almost completely extinguished and economic life became subservient to the reigning ideology. This social structure represents repression.

In spite of the tremendous power wielded in both systems by the state, its subjection in one case by the economic sphere and in the other by ideology, has nearly obliterated its true nature. Both societies have authoritarian systems. The economy rules in the West, ideology in the East. The former has a more aggressive character while the latter is more repressive. It could also be said that the two systems have opposing associations of thinking and willing. In the West the strong will of economic power uses as its tool a technical, mechanistic way of thinking. In the East ideological thinking uses as its tool the strong will of socio-political power. Neither leaves room for the realm of feeling. But it is out of this that society develops its feeling for the sphere of rights. And it is the essential task of the state to bring this sphere of rights into existence. If this could be done, then the present exclusive rule of *power* would be tempered by that of *rights*. Then the systems of the West and the East would be dismantled and their contrasting difference balanced out. Modern states do, it is true, make laws, but these are not dictated by a sense of what is right, but simply by who is in power. What is regarded as 'right' is what is right in law, even if it is not in keeping with what is felt to be right. It springs from a nominalistic view and not a realistic one.

It is true that on the basis of natural rights - the law of reason - human rights were first declared in America in the 18th century. They were formulated anew, first in France and then in the present century by the United Nations Organisation. Nowhere, however, have they achieved legal enforcement. The enslavement of the state, by the economic sphere on the one hand, and of the national state by socialist ideology on the other hand, has prevented this. The modern states claim to be democracies, but all this concept has stood for since the declaration of human rights has so far not been fully realised anywhere. For the essential requirement of democracy is the principle of equal rights for human beings. But so far this has only existed in theory. It could only be realised if the state, instead of representing the Roman conception of universality, were to aim at being the mediator between the economic and the cultural life, i.e. between the principles of individuality and universality. While in the West the state became the servant of private economic interests, in the East it remained the representative of common interests; it has been pushed and pulled in opposite directions and so distorted that it has been unable to realise the principle of equality of rights. Outside forces - either economic or cultural - are always at work damaging the citizens' equal rights. The state should have made itself independent of economic and cultural interests and confined itself exclusively to its fundamental task of ordering and safeguarding rights. The equality of rights, which the democratic state is obliged to realise, applies not only between individuals but also between the individual and society. If the rights of the individual preponderate, society is in danger of disintegrating into a mere sum of individuals (as is the tendency in the West). If the opposite occurs, there is the danger, as has happened in the East, that the private sphere is wiped out and the individual is completely absorbed into society. Such violations of equal rights are the results of the fusion of the state with either the economic or the cultural realm.

Equality of rights means that not only does everyone enjoy equal rights but also that everyone has the same right to be actively engaged in apportioning them. This requires a much greater degree of participation of all citizens in legislation than is customary in the parliamentary system, for this is not concerned with rights, but rather with the furthering of largely economic interests and the gaining of positions of power. Hence in most 'democracies' the participation of all citizens is limited to the electing of parliamentary representatives. If everyone has an equal right to share in determining matters, then of course only such things can be voted on which every sound, mentally-balanced adult can decide out of his feeling for what is right. Everything requiring special knowledge in the cultural or economic realms must be excluded. In the present time, with knowledge far more specialised than it has ever been, it would be an injustice to the experts if everyone had an equal right to vote on matters requiring expert knowledge. Today questions are decided by referendum and in parliament which far exceed the knowledge and capacity of judgment of the voters. Besides this, expertise and discrimination are confused intentionally in election campaigns by propaganda and counter-propaganda. The individual can do no more than cast his vote according to egotistic interests or party slogans. In this way the instinctive sense of what is right is more and more blunted and eventually silenced.

For the sake of the state itself the cultural and economic spheres ought to organise themselves according to *their* diverse functions so that the state can fulfill *its* task. Only to the extent that it can do so will the struggle between ideology and economy decline, so that simultaneously with the *synthesis* of the individual and the universal there can also be a *balancing* between them at a higher level and in a new form. Here a third way opens - a third alternative between the two false paths of the contemporary social systems of West and East.

The potential for this alternative did exist in central Europe. Wilhelm von Humboldt pointed the way as early on as the time of the French Revolution in his work *Thoughts on an Endeavour to Determine the Limits of State Action* (1792).

After the First World War Rudolf Steiner advocated it in a more developed form as the idea of the Threefold

Social Order. The rejection of this idea led Germany to succumb to its opposite - National Socialism - which is not a synthesis but a mere chaotic mixture of western and eastern liberal and social, aggressive and repressive tendencies. It led to the explosion of the Second World War followed by the political division of the country whose parts became integrated into the social systems and power blocs of the West and the East. The present conditions in Central Europe cannot last but are drifting inevitably towards a third catastrophy. The 'German Question' is not solved. More than any other part of the world - owing to its geographical position - Central Europe can only become socially sound and whole to the extent that a new threefold social order is established on its soil. An attempt to show the sequence of steps to be taken along this path has been made in this book.

It remains to point out that through a threefold ordering of society a synthesis and thus a new equilibrium between the principles of individuality and universality of a different kind can also be achieved: namely in respect of the relationship between man and the universe.

In the first main epoch of man's development, the principle of universality held sway, as explained in the fourth chapter. In Paradise man as microcosm was still in original universal union with God and nature. This union was preserved, though in a new form, far on into the second epoch.

In the course of this second epoch, individualism came more and more to the fore until finally it turned the balance and became completely one-sided. Man cut himself loose from God and nature; he set himself against God and denied him, and became the destroyer of nature. Today he finds himself completely isolated, 'he encounters only himself' (Heisenberg) and feels as if cast into the void. His existence has lost all meaning. He is threatened with ruin through self-annihilation, both by the destruction of his physical basis of existence and by the complete loss of moral standards (which were based on religion) entailing moral nihilism, i.e. unchecked, all-against-all aggression. In the form of society today this is expressed in the administrative bunching together of the cultural and economic life in a uniform or total state, which subjects everything to politics, and thus extinguishes and wipes out the real nature of the state, which is to formulate and safeguard the true ordering of rights.

A cultural life which can order its own affairs and is free to devote itself to its own tasks, especially today the development of a true science of man, will, through doing so, open up a new approach to the divine, spiritual world. In the universally human which this science awakens in the individual, man will find that universal being which makes him aware that he is of the same nature as the divine. No longer, through religious faith, does he feel himself an immature child of God, but he knows then that he has come of age as the son and partner of the divinity. An intimate dialogue evolves between the two, a mutual giving and taking, which endows the cultural life with a new creativity and moral strength for the shaping of individual and social life.

As long as man experienced himself as an immature child of God, he felt obliged to submit to His guidance, be obedient to His commandments and offer sacrifice. As he lost this link and became estranged from the divine, he felt himself maturing, and seeing himself confronted by material nature, he believed that he had to demonstrate and prove his maturity by making himself its master; but he became more and more its exploiter and destroyer. If he attains a new relationship to the divine, in freedom, conscious of being of the same divine essence, he will inevitably gain a new relationship to nature. If he sees the divinity no longer as only his father and lord but learns to know the incarnate Son of God as his brother, then he will realise that nature is not a maid serving him, but a mother nourishing him and that the rest of creation are his brothers and sisters. His sense of responsibility for nature will then be awakened - not least in relation to his own survival.

The economy, when freely administering its own affairs, will not only socialise the relationship of man to man but will develop an attitude to nature through which the destruction inevitably wrought by technology can be healed and made good by appropriate means.

Finally in the sphere of rights (the state), as shown earlier, the individual will respect his fellow men and treat them as equals. Thus true humanity will enter political life.

All this will bring about the synthesis of the principles of individuality and universality - also in their cosmic sense.

In such a threefold society mankind will remain the independent third world, between the divine and natural worlds, into which humanity has matured in the course of history. With regard to the universal cosmos, the principle of universality thus remains valid. Through the threefold ordering, human society, having become independent, will show a truly human face.

Conversely the new relationship to the divine, spiritual world in the sphere of cultural life, and to material nature in the economic sphere, will unite man with the universe; in fact man and the world will become again a universal whole.

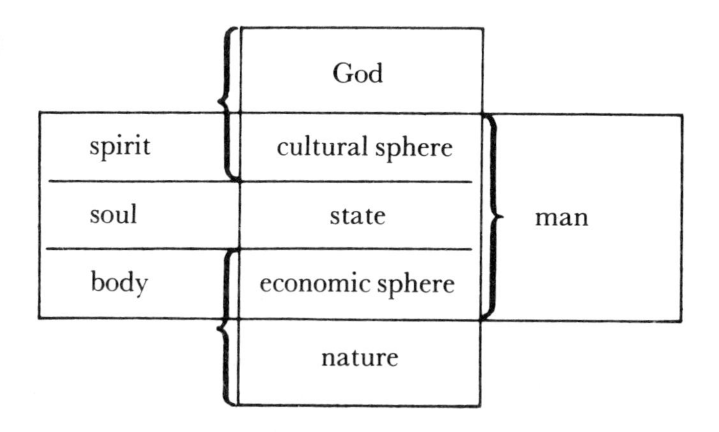

The diagram illustrates this synthesis of the two principles.

The threefoldness of human society reveals itself as a

microcosm, a counterpart to the threefold macrocosm embracing the divine, mankind and nature. In the course of developing towards this new awareness, man acquires the certainty that both as an individual and as the whole of society he only takes his appropriate and rightful place within the universe if he stands between the divine and nature, acting constantly as their mediator and holding the balance. In order to do this the individual needs to experience himself as a threefold being of body, soul and spirit; and society needs to interlink the functions of the three spheres - economic, state (rights) and cultural. It is the only way to restore the balance which is so disturbed today - in the West by the predominating power of the economy, in the East by that of ideology. Both deprive man of the possibility of achieving true humanity.

This fact clearly shows the interdependence and mutual responsibility that exist between the individual and society. The individual can unfold his truly human nature only in a humanised society, in the way described. And the humanising of society depends on that of the individual. Being human entails an active participation in the ordering and administration of all three spheres of society. This points to the difference between Graeco-Roman antiquity and modern times. Then man felt fully human when he was active in the sphere of both private and public rights, i.e. as a private person and as a citizen. In future he will feel human only when he participates responsibly in all three spheres - the economic, the political and the cultural. This means that the individual will have to be socially involved more widely than he usually is today, when he is generally only interested in the sphere of his profession. A person is, however, not merely a professional specialist; he is also a human being. He will in the future have to acknowledge and practise his humanity far more consciously in all its implications if society is to become more human. Only this will bring about something that it is feared might be lost through the abolition of the authoritarian state: the *unity* of the threefold social order. This will be realised in a new way in *every individual* to the degree of his active involvement in all spheres of a society which, in its turn, makes this involvement possible through its threefold ordering. The individual human being will become infinitely more important for the life of society than he can now be under the rulership of an omnipotent state, which condemns him to sink ever deeper into a condition of social impotence.

We live today at the time of one of the greatest turning points of human evolution. We all feel this in some way. The new development, which must occur if there is to be a future, cannot be had for a price less than that set out in these chapters. What is required is a new value and meaning of human existence. For the destiny of mankind will be decided at the present turning point in evolution.

Bibliography

Behrendt, R.F.
Der Mensch im Lichte der Soziologie, Stuttgart 1962

Carrel, A.
Man, The Unknown, London 1935

Gehlen, A.
Der Mensch, seine Natur und seine Stellung in der Welt, 1950

Jaspers, K.
Vom Ursprung und Sinn der Geschichte, Zurich 1949

Jores, A.
Menschsein im Auftrag, Bern 1967

Lorenz, K.
On Aggression, London 1966

Lüthy, H.
Die Mathematisierung der Sozialwissenschaften, Zurich 1970

Mitscherlich, A.
Society without the Father, London 1969

Rattner, J.
Aggression und menschliche Natur, Olten 1970

Scheler, M.
Die Stellung des Menschen im Kosmos, Darmstadt 1928

Selg, H.
Making of Human Aggression: A Psychological Approach, London 1975

Skinner, B.F.
Beyond Freedom and Dignity, London 1972

Steiner, R.
The Philosophy of Freedom, London 1979
Towards Social Renewal, London 1977
Neugestaltung des sozialen Organismus, Dornach 1963

Wagner, F.
Die Wissenschaft und die gefährdete Welt, Munich 1964

Wehr, G.
C.G. Jung und Rudolf Steiner, Stuttgart 1972

Pharos
paperback series

THE PHILOSOPHY OF FREEDOM
A basis for a modern world conception
Rudolf Steiner
272pp. ISBN 0 85440 350 7

OCCULT SCIENCE
An Outline
Rudolf Steiner
352pp. ISBN 0 85440 349 3

LIVING WITH YOUR BODY
Walther Bühler M.D.
128pp. ISBN 0 85440 345 0

THE WAY OF A CHILD
A.C. Harwood
144pp. ISBN 0 85440 352 3

RUDOLF STEINER EDUCATION
The Waldorf Schools
Francis Edmunds
144pp. ISBN 0 85440 344 2

THE EVOLUTION OF CONSCIOUSNESS
Rudolf Steiner
208pp. ISBN 0 85440 351 5

PHASES
Crisis and Development in the Individual
Bernard Lievegoed M.D.
256pp. ISBN 0 85440 353 1

Further titles in preparation.